Signposts in Economics

Peter Rigby

Nelson

Thomas Nelson and Sons Ltd
Nelson House Mayfield Road
Walton-on-Thames Surrey
KT12 5PL UK

51 York Place
Edinburgh
EH1 3JD UK

Thomas Nelson (Hong Kong) Ltd
Toppan Building 10/F
22a Westlands Road
Quarry Bay Hong Kong

Thomas Nelson Australia
102 Dodds Street
South Melbourne
Victoria 3205 Australia

Nelson Canada
1120 Birchmount Road
Scarborough Ontario
M1K 5G4 Canada

© Peter Rigby 1987

First published by Macmillan Education Ltd 1987
(under ISBN 0-333-42274-0)

This edition published by Thomas Nelson and Sons Ltd 1992

ISBN 0-17-438617-6
NPN 9 8 7 6 5 4 3

Printed in Hong Kong.

Acknowledgements

The author and publishers wish to thank the following who has kindly
given permission for the use of copyright material: the *Guardian* for
extracts from 'BHS deal puts City in fever' by G. Gibbs & A. Cornelius
(27.11.85) and 'Taxman "ignores" black economy' by A. Rawnsley
(27.11.85).

The author and publishers wish to acknowledge the following photograph
sources: ASA Ltd, p. 16; Camera Press, pp. 4, 23, 24; J. Allan Cash Ltd,
pp. 4, 29, 31 (right), 34, 41 (lower); Derbyshire County Council, pp. 32,
33; Chris Fairclough, p. 1; Good Relations, p. 20; Lancashire Evening
Post, p. 17; Marc, p. 21; Midland Bank PLC, pp. 10, 14; National Coal
Board, p. 7; Popperfoto, p. 31 (left); Press Association Ltd, p. 39; Ken
Pyne, p. 27; Rex Features, p. 41 (top); Sociology Update, p. 5; John
Topham Picture Library, p. 8; West Yorkshire Metropolitan County
Council, p. 33.

Every effort has been made to trace all the copyright holders but if any
have been inadvertently overlooked the publishers will be pleased to make
the necessary arrangement at the first opportunity.

Contents

Introduction

On a car journey or walk through a town centre, we can see many signposts at the roadside. They provide general directions to travellers. Signposts point people in the right direction and inform them which route to take.

In the same way, the *Signposts* series of books is designed to provide you with basic information about the society you live in. The *Signposts* books will guide you towards an understanding of the main institutions and organisations in society and how they work. *Signposts* books will be useful in helping you to identify the most important topics that concern society today. I hope that you will enjoy reading them, using them, and learning from them.

Dr Lynton Robins

Unit One
What is economics?

What do you need to live happily?

Which needs are these people satisfying?

We all have different needs and want different things; but we do not have enough money to buy everything we want.

How do we decide what things we will buy with our money? We put our wants and needs in some sort of order. This is called a **scale of preference**. The things we want most will go to the top of the list. The things we want badly but not quite so much, go next, and so on.

Money is important in our lives. Why do you think the well-known saying goes 'The love of money is the root of all evil'? People don't usually want money for its own sake. They need it for the things they can buy with it.

Imagine that you have been given £5.00. You have got certain choices open to you. Do you:

- Go to a disco or go to the cinema?
- Buy some records or buy some clothes?
- Keep it in your pocket or put it in a savings account?

What should I do with my £5?

You have many choices open to you, but the amount of money you have to spend is limited. Money, like all other resources, is scarce. This problem of scarcity and choice lies at the heart of economics.

RESOURCES (scarce) \ / NEEDS AND WANTS (unlimited)
THE ECONOMIC PROBLEM

Imagine that you decide to spend your £5.00 on a ticket for a rock concert. Once you have bought your ticket you haven't any money left to spend on records, magazines and so on. You have made a decision to do without these other items in order to go to the concert. In economics, this is known as **opportunity cost**.

One person's necessity may be another person's luxury. It is all a matter of how much we feel we can afford – that is, how much we can spend to satisfy our wants. A millionaire with all his or her wealth is likely to have many more wants than an individual with an average income. A poor person in Britain will have different wants from those of someone living in poverty in the

Third World. The resources that each will have to satisfy his or her wants will be different too.

The study of wants/needs and resources is what economics is about. It may be used to consider how individuals, firms and governments face the same basic problem – that is, of deciding how much to spend and which wants to satisfy.

Workshop   Workshop   Workshop

1 What does an economist mean by:
   (a) Wants
   (b) Resources
   (c) Scale of preference
   (d) Price
   (e) Opportunity cost?

2 What are basic necessities and luxuries to you? Make two lists of those items you consider necessities and those that you would call luxuries.

3 (a) Keep a diary of your spending for a weekend. List in two columns:
       (i) The items you bought and how much they cost
       (ii) The money you received or earned
   (b) How did you decide to spend your money?
   (c) Are there any items you have had to do without?
   (d) How much money have you got left at the end of the weekend?

Patterns of household expenditure in Britain, 1980 (percentages)

4 (a) Copy out the paragraph below in full, filling in the blank spaces from the list of words given at the bottom. Use the information in the graph to help you.

A middle-income household has just under _____ as much money to spend as a low-income household. A high-income household has nearly _____ times as much to spend. Low-income families spend proportionately more on basic necessities such as _____, _____ and _____ _____ _____. All households spend approximately the same proportions on _____ _____ _____ and _____ _____ _____. However, the most noticeable differences concern luxury items, _____ _____ _____ and _____ _____ _____ on which middle- and high-income families spend twice as much of their money.

twice   fuel and light   transport and vehicles
food   housing   clothing and footwear
alcohol and tobacco   three   durable household goods

(Note: Durable household goods include items such as television sets, cookers, washing machines, furniture, carpets and fridges.)

   (b) Which items would be included in the category entitled 'Other'?

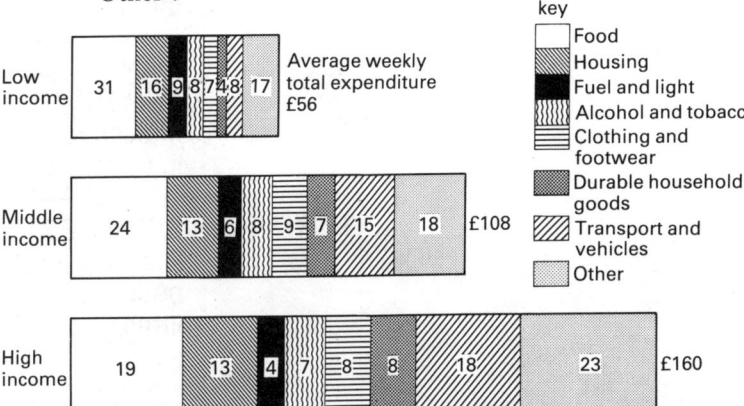

key
☐ Food
▨ Housing
■ Fuel and light
▥ Alcohol and tobacco
▤ Clothing and footwear
▦ Durable household goods
▨ Transport and vehicles
▨ Other

Low income: 31 16 9 8 7 4 8 17   Average weekly total expenditure £56

Middle income: 24 13 6 8 9 7 15 18   £108

High income: 19 13 4 7 8 8 18 23   £160

3

Unit Two
Work and unemployment

The **working population** consists of men aged from sixteen to sixty-five and women aged sixteen to sixty – this includes both full- and part-time workers.

In 1984, the working population of Britain totalled 27 062 000 of whom sixty-five per cent were male and thirty-five per cent female.

Where do people work?

Industries and occupations can be divided into three major types:

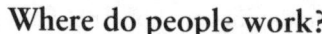

Primary   Secondary   Tertiary

TYPE	MEANING	EXAMPLES	PERCEN-TAGE OF WORKING POPULA-TION
PRIMARY	EXTRACTIVE Taking re-sources from the earth	Farming Fishing Mining	3.2
SECON-DARY	MANUFAC-TURING Making goods in factories	Steel Chemicals Electronics	39.4
TERTIARY	SERVICES Provided for people and firms	Shops and offices Council employees Banks and insurance	57.3

Today, increasing numbers of women work. Many work in service industries like banking. Services are the fastest growing type of employment in Britain

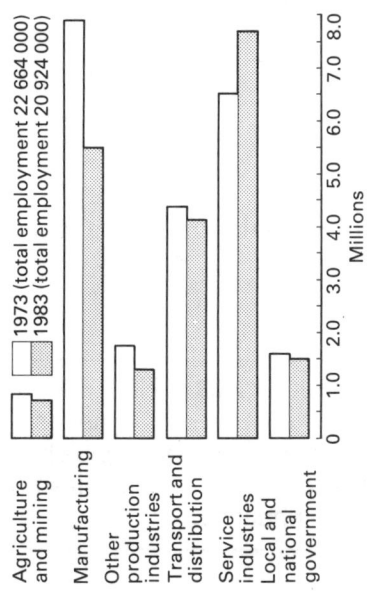

Employees in employment in Britain

Can you think of any more examples for each category?

Over the last twenty years changes have taken place in the types of work done by the working population:

1 Fewer people work in primary and secondary industries, while there has been a sharp rise in service industries.
2 There are now many more women in the work-force.
3 More people work part-time, most of them women. Six per cent of male employees are part-time, while the proportion of women part-time workers is forty-two per cent.
4 Workers enjoy longer holidays and a shorter working week. But unemployment is a major social problem in Britain in the 1980s. The number of people out of work has increased sharply from 1.2 million in 1979 to 3.4 million in January 1986.

The groups most affected by unemployment are:

YOUNG PEOPLE   BLACK PEOPLE
UNQUALIFIED AND UNSKILLED PEOPLE

Workshop   Workshop   Workshop

1 What do you understand by the terms:
   (a) Working population
   (b) Secondary industries
   (c) Service industries?

2 From the information given in the graph:
   (a) Which is the only industry to show an increase between the years 1973 and 1983?
   (b) Which type of industry has shown the greatest decrease?
   (c) Which industry employed most people in 1973?
   (d) Which industry employed most people in 1983?

3 Draw a graph to show the percentages of workers in primary, secondary and tertiary industries.

4 From the information provided on the chart and map:
   (a) Construct a table to show unemployment in the regions of Britain. Put the region with the highest unemployment at the top and the region with the lowest at the bottom.
   (b) In which part of Britain is the lowest rate of unemployment?
   (c) What do you think the term 'long-term unemployment' means?
   (d) Which three age-groups have the highest number of unemployed people?
   (e) Why are so few people in the sixty-and-over age-group unemployed?

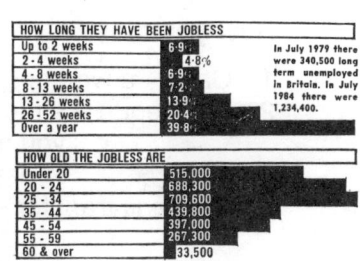

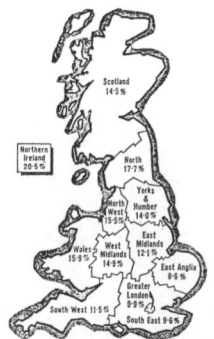

Unemployment in Britain

5

Unit Three
Wages

When you are working, you will probably receive a pay advice slip on pay day.

Name:		Payroll number	
W/Beg:		Tax Code:	
Basic Pay	Overtime		**Total Gross Pay**
Deductions			
NI	Tax	Pension	Union	Saving	**Total Deductions**
					Net Pay
DELICIOUS CAKES LTD			£

A pay slip

TOTAL GROSS PAY	−	TOTAL DEDUCTIONS	=	NET PAY
means Money earned including overtime		means Taxes, National Insurance and pensions contributions		means Money actually received

You may be paid either weekly or monthly. A **wage** is calculated on an hourly or weekly basis and is paid weekly. A **salary** is calculated as an annual amount which is then divided into twelve roughly equal monthly payments. Basic or normal pay is called the **wage rate**. Extra amounts may be earned through bonus payments and overtime pay. The total amount that a person is paid, including all overtime and bonus, is known as **earnings**. Most workers earn an amount which has been calculated hourly, weekly, monthly or annually. This is called a **time-rate** – that is, so much for a given time spent at work.

Alternatively, wages and earnings may be calculated according to the amount a person actually produces. The more you produce, the more you are paid. This is called a **piece-rate**.

How you may be paid

1 Cash – a worker is paid in notes and coin.
2 By cheque – a more secure and convenient method, but you must have a bank account or be able to cash the cheque elsewhere.
3 By credit transfer – neither money nor cheque changes hands. Pay goes directly into a bank account. Very convenient for the employer and a secure method of payment.

High wages may have to be paid for dangerous and 'dirty' jobs

What determines wage rates and earnings?

LEVEL OF SKILL	More highly skilled workers can usually get higher wage rates.
EDUCATION AND TRAINING	The length of education and training often results in higher levels of pay.
JOB ATTRACTIVENESS	People may not want to do 'dirty' jobs, so high wages have to be paid. Unsocial hours may also be unpopular.
TRADE UNION ACTIVITY	Trade union power may result in certain groups of workers earning above-average rates of pay.

Workshop　　Workshop　　Workshop

1 What do you understand by
   (a) Wages
   (b) Salaries
   (c) Earnings
   (d) Deductions?

2 What are the main differences between time-rates and piece-rates?

3 Can you think of any groups of workers who cannot be paid by piece-rates?

4 Select one type of job. Outline its most attractive and unattractive features. State whether it is usually highly paid or poorly paid. Explain the reason for your answer.

Britain's pay and hours (full-time employees whose pay was not affected by absence, April 1984)

	Male	Female	Manual	Non-manual
Average gross earnings (including overtime)	£178.80	£117.20	£143.00.	£172.20
Average total weekly hours (including overtime)	41.7	37.2	43.5	37.6
Gross earnings per hour (including overtime)	£4.29	£3.15	£3.29	£4.58

5 (a) Compare the levels of:
       (i) Male and female wages
       (ii) Manual and non-manual workers' wages
   (b) Suggest reasons why males earn more than females.
   (c) Why do males tend to work longer hours each week than females?
   (d) Why do you think non-manual wages are higher than manual workers' wages?

7

Unit Four
Trade unions

The first factories in Britain were built during the Industrial Revolution, in the late eighteenth and early nineteenth centuries. Working conditions were often appalling. Hours were long, jobs hard and often dangerous; injuries and deaths at work were commonplace. These early factory workers had no freedom to organise themselves into societies or trade unions to protect themselves from poor management.

The first trade unions were set up for skilled workers during the 1850s and 1860s, but they had very little real power until the Trade Union Acts of 1871 and 1875. These Acts gave the unions legal status, protected their funds and legalised peaceful picketing.

However most unskilled workers were not represented until the end of the nineteenth century. Many of these early unions have since merged to create larger, more powerful, general unions – the total number of trade unions fell from 453 in 1979 to 401 in 1982. The largest unions in Britain today are the Transport and General Workers Union and the General Municipal Workers and Boilermakers Union.

Since the 1960s the greatest growth in union membership has been amongst 'white-collar workers' – for example, technicians, office workers, teachers, civil servants and health service workers.

Working conditions in many factories during the nineteenth century were often appalling

What does a union provide for its workers?

- Seeks better rates of pay.
- Tries to improve working conditions.
- Provides sports and social facilities.
- Gives legal advice.
- Assists with compensation schemes for workers who have been dismissed or lost pay through strike action.

The organisation of unions

Unions are democratically organised bodies; this means that National Executive members and the General Secretary are elected and are full-time paid officials. The

Under a closed shop agreement, non-union members usually will not be employed

rights of individual union members are protected by locally elected shop stewards. Negotiations at work are carried out between the management and the shop stewards representing the union members.

Most major unions are members of the Trades Union Congress. Congress meets once a year to discuss trade union policies. As an organisation, it represents the views of the trade union movement to the employers and the government. It also helps to settle disputes between its member trade unions.

Joining a trade union

You cannot be forced to join a union unless a 'closed shop' agreement exists between the union and management. In this case you have to be a union member as a condition of your employment. Members pay a subscription which goes towards the running costs of the union.

Workshop   Workshop   Workshop

1 Why were trade unions formed after the Industrial Revolution?

2

Membership of selected trade unions for 1979 and 1982 (in thousands)			
	1979	1982	percentage change
Transport and General Workers Union	2086	1633	−21.7
Amalgamated Union of Engineering Workers	1510	1242	−17.7
Associated Society of Technical and Managerial Staffs	491	410	−16.5
National Union of Teachers	291	260	−10.7
National Association of Local Government Officers	753	726	−3.6
National Union of Public Employees	692	702	+1.4
Confederation of Health Service Employees	213	232	+8.9
Royal College of Nursing	162	223	+37.7

(a) Look at the membership figures of unions representing workers in manufacturing industry. What happened between 1979 and 1982? Suggest reasons for this change.

(b) In contrast, what happened to the membership figures in the public sector? Why do you think this occurred?

3 Follow the progress of an industrial dispute by collecting newspaper articles to build up a file of information.
Find out in particular:
The main areas of disagreement between employer and union.
The length of time the dispute lasted.
How it was eventually settled.

9

Unit Five
Spending

How do we buy goods and services?

How can we pay for the goods in the trolley?

Notes and coins are the most common method of payment. These are issued through the banks. The Royal Mint produces or 'mints' coins, and banknotes are printed by the Bank of England.

If you have a bank account you may find that a cheque is a more convenient way of paying. To prevent fraud, nearly all shops and services require you to produce a cheque card, which guarantees that the bank will honour cheques up to a certain value.

If you don't have a bank account, postal orders can be bought from the post office. These can be used for buying goods by mail order.

If you have a regular income and are 'credit-worthy', you can apply for a credit card. **Credit** means buying now and paying later.

Buying with the use of credit facilities is a form of borrowing. The main types of credit are as follows:

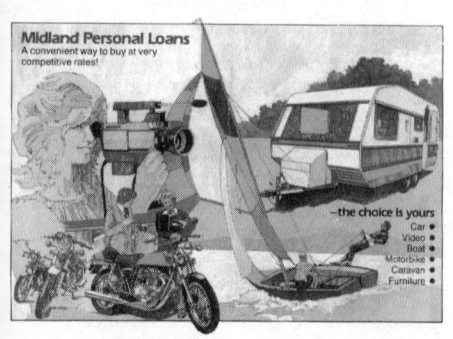

10

TYPE OF CREDIT	ADVANTAGES	DISADVAN-TAGES
CREDIT CARD Provided by a credit company. Allows you to buy goods and pay for them later.	Acceptable at many shops. Convenient and easy to carry. Can be used in emergencies.	If you lose your card, it may be used dishonestly by someone else. High interest rate charged.
HIRE PURCHASE With this type of credit you don't own the goods until you make your final payment.	A useful way to buy goods if you haven't a bank account or credit card.	Rate of interest charged is higher than a bank charges its customers.
PERSONAL LOAN A bank lends you a sum of money for a specific purpose. You repay this sum over a certain period.	Available if you have a bank account. You know how much you will have to repay each month and the amount of interest charged.	Only available if you have a secure job (regular income) and if the bank trusts your ability to repay.
OVERDRAFT Means that your current account is 'in the red'. The bank usually requires you to pay back quickly.	Interest only paid on money owed to the bank. A useful way of borrowing for a short time.	Current account with a bank is required. Strict limit is imposed on the amount borrowed.

When you repay a loan, **interest** is charged on top of the original amount borrowed. This is the cost of borrowing the money and represents a reward or payment to the lender.

Workshop   Workshop   Workshop

1 What do you understand by:
   (a) Bank account
   (b) Credit card
   (c) Personal loan
   (d) Overdraft?

2 Which methods of buying goods are open to you:
   (a) If you have a bank account?
   (b) If you don't have a bank account?

3 Why do you have to pay interest on borrowed money?

4 Could you take out a bank loan if you wanted to? Find out from your local bank or post office.

Unit Six
Prices

How are prices worked out?

Who works out what the prices should be on this stall?

Prices are decided by the forces of demand and supply. These are **market forces**. A market exists when people who wish to buy (the demand) come together with people who have goods for sale (the supply).

The market in your nearest town or city is an example of this process. You can 'shop around' and try to get a bargain, that is the best value for money. Major centres have markets dealing in specialised products. Here are some examples in London:

MARKET NAME	DEALING IN
The Stock Exchange	Stocks and shares
New Smithfield	Meat
New Covent Garden	Fruit, vegetables and flowers
Hatton Garden	Diamonds

Can you think of any other examples?

Economists identify special conditions which, when they happen, enable a perfect market to exist.

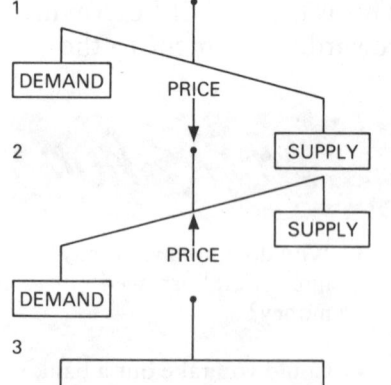

How prices are determined

The conditions are:

1   There are a large number of buyers and sellers.
2   The goods for sale are considered to be identical.
3   Anyone may buy the goods offered for sale.
4   Ownership may be easily transferred to the buyer.

Under conditions of a perfect market, prices are fixed where the amount that people are willing to buy (DEMAND) equals the quantity which people are prepared to sell (SUPPLY).

Let's look at the factors affecting demand and supply.

DEMAND	SUPPLY
Seasonal factors	Weather conditions
Climate	
Fashion	Costs of raw materials, fuel and wages
Changes in public tastes	Taxes imposed by the government
Prices of competing goods	Prices of alternative goods (substitutes)
Levels of incomes	

When the factors affecting demand or supply change, then the price at which the goods are offered for sale will also be affected.

Workshop   *Workshop*   *Workshop*

1   What does an economist mean by:
    (a) A market
    (b) Demand
    (c) Supply?

2   What will happen to prices if:
    (a) Demand exceeds supply
    (b) Supply exceeds demand
    (c) Demand equals supply?

3   What would happen to the price of carrots if:
    (a) The ground was frozen, preventing farmers from harvesting their crops
    (b) The cost of diesel fuel for lorries doubled
    (c) There was a particularly good harvest, producing a glut of carrots?

4   Taxes are often imposed by the government to raise money. They also have the effect of increasing the price of a good.

    What could the government do if it wished to encourage people to use more of a particular good?

Unit Seven
Saving

Does money burn a hole in your pocket or can you set some aside for a rainy day?

Why do we save?

- For things we can't afford straightaway.
- In case of emergency.
- To increase our money by letting it earn interest.

Most banks have set up savings accounts particularly to attract young savers

Once you have made up your mind to save, you have to decide on the best place to put your money. You could hide it under your mattress, but there are safer and more profitable places to keep it. Building societies and banks are keen for you to save with them. Many make tempting offers such as free gifts or higher interest rates in the hope that you will continue to keep an account with them throughout your life.

Your neighbourhood post office also offers a local alternative in the form of a National Savings account.

Deciding on the best place for your savings can be a real problem

What are the risks of saving?

If **inflation** is high, your savings may lose value in real terms.

How are you encouraged to save?

You can gain interest on your savings. This helps you to beat inflation – but only if interest rates are higher than the rate of inflation.

What happens to your money?

Banks – lend money to industry, the government and customers in the form of overdrafts and personal loans.
Building societies – lend money to house purchasers in the form of mortgages.
National Savings – goes to pay for government spending.

Workshop   Workshop   Workshop

1   Explain why people save money.

2   What do you understand by:
(a) 'Saving for a rainy day'
(b) Inflation
(c) National Savings
(d) Mortgage?

3   The table below shows types of savings in 1983.
(a) Show this information in a graph.
(b) Which of these types of savings represent a loan to the government?

4   Collect information about different methods of saving from local banks, building societies and the post office.

Draw up a table to compare the various types under the following headings:
Type   Interest paid
Conditions
Other comments

Percentage of adults holding:			
Bank current account	Bank deposit account	National Savings Bank account	Trustee Savings Bank account
61	32	15	14
Building society account	Premium Savings Bonds	National Savings Bonds	Stocks and shares
57	44	12	11

Unit Eight
Advertising and consumer protection

Looking for a bargain? You might be able to pick up what you need cheaply in the Classified Advertisements section of your local newspaper.

Goods are advertised as new or second-hand. Some advertisements merely tell you about goods available while others try to persuade you to buy.

Some salesmen may use dishonest methods to persuade you to buy from them

But what can we do if we suspect that an advertisement is misleading, or telling downright lies?

First of all you can complain at your local Citizens' Advice Bureau. You will find the nearest office listed in the phone book. They will tell you whether you have got a case if the matter needs taking to court.

Laws have been passed by Parliament to protect **consumers** from unscrupulous traders and advertisers.

The Advertising Standards Authority controls all aspects of advertising in Britain, and helps to ensure that the advertisements seen and heard on TV, radio and in newspapers and magazines are not misleading and, as far as possible, tell the truth.

Consumers are also protected by law when buying goods from shops. Shops cannot make you keep faulty or shoddy goods and they have to ensure that weighing equipment is accurate. But there are subtle ways in which advertisers encourage us to spend, for example:

- by making extravagant claims
- through special offers and 'free' gifts
- by appealing to our vanity
- by encouraging us to 'keep up with the Jones's'

Today, advertising is a multi-million-pound industry. So think before you buy and remember that laws exist to protect the consumer.

Workshop   Workshop   Workshop

1 Study these advertisements which are taken from a local newspaper.

ARTICLES FOR SALE

FANTASTIC OPPORTUNITY — BUT HURRY!!

UNBELIEVABLE CLEARANCE PRICES

on electronic organs and keyboards, Combo/Leslie cabinets, musical instruments, stereos, quality leather and dralon lounge furniture. Also pre-owned suites from £15!!

DEFINITELY YOUR LAST OPPORTUNITY TO BUY AT CLEARANCE PRICES.

PRESTIGE CLEARING WAREHOUSE 3 MARSH LANE

Entrance off Friargate, adjacent 4 Mat Computer

Open 10 am - 8 pm (Car parking facilities)

SALE BY CATALOGUE KEN

Fantastic selection of goods including ladies dresses, knitwear, gents and children's wear, plus many other autumn and winter items and toys too numerous to mention.

All to be sold at absolutely silly prices!!

Sale to be held at
SCHOOL LANE
WORKING MEN'S CLUB
Bamber Bridge, on
THURSDAY, NOVEMBER 28
Starting at 7 30 pm prompt.

DECORATE FOR CHRISTMAS

Thousands of bargains in paint and wallpaper.

QUEENS MILL
RIPON STREET, PRESTON

Late Opening 8 pm Mon-Fri
Sat 10-5, Sun 10-4

MOULINEX Rotisserie £25; Camp kitchen £7; Coney and leather dark brown jacket, size 12 £10; White metal cord pull curtain rail, adjustable in length, 12ft approx. £10; Green Dralon and chrome swivel stool, £15.

ITEMS FOR SALE: piano and stool, £65; Video (Betamax), £195; lounge suite (3 piece Chesterfield, Dralon), £150; dining suite, £35; snooker table with accessories, 6ft x 3ft, £50.

DELUSO, fully fitted kitchen work top, sink and mixer taps, never been used, £500 o.n.o.

BARBIE'S Star Traveller, Barbie's car, moped and canopy bed. All in good condition, £45.

GENT'S BIKE, three speed, hub wheel dynamo, £70; Sunbed, in pine, £100; child's Bontempi Organ, as new, still in box, £35.

(a) What does 'o.n.o.' mean?
(b) Give another way of describing 'pre-owned suites'.

(c) Most of the advertisements are for second-hand goods; which ones are selling new articles?

2 Collect advertisements from magazines and national or local newspapers.
   (a) Separate those which are only informing you from those which are designed to persuade you to buy a product or service.
   (b) What methods are the advertisers using in attempting to get us to spend our money?
   (c) Discuss any other advertising methods you know.

3 Have you ever had to complain about a product? Explain what happened. Discuss what you could or should have done.

4 Find out more about the Advertising Standards Authority. Write to the address in their advertisement to get your copy of the Advertising Code of Practice.

17

Unit Nine

Organisation and finance of firms

An **entrepreneur** is someone who runs a business enterprise or firm. That person is responsible for:

MAKING DECISIONS	TAKING RISKS

If these decisions prove to be correct ones and if the risks taken are successful, the firm makes a **profit**. If not, it makes a **loss**.

Not all firms are large. They vary tremendously in size. Here are the main types of firms:

1 SOLE PROPRIETOR: a business run by one person which is usually fairly inexpensive to set up (for example, small shopkeepers, window cleaners).
2 PARTNERSHIP: a slightly larger firm owned by between two and twenty people. A sole proprietor wishing to expand the business may invite other people to put money into it and join as partners, so sharing the profits. Partnerships are often found in the professions – architects, dentists, doctors and solicitors, for example. However, a firm's size may be limited by the amount of money partners are willing to invest and the bank is prepared to lend.
3 PRIVATE JOINT STOCK COMPANY: this may be the answer for a firm wishing to expand. It can have up to fifty people who own shares in the business. Ordinary members of the public cannot buy these shares except by invitation from the company's directors.
4 PUBLIC LIMITED COMPANY (PLC): generally the largest type of company. Shares are bought and sold on the Stock Exchange to anyone willing and able to buy them. Professional managers are appointed to run the firm. These people take decisions, while the

The risks for the entrepreneur are considerable

shareholders take the risks. The shareholders are invited to an annual meeting to hear the company reports and to elect members of the Board of Directors who, in turn, appoint the top managers. The law requires PLCs to publish their accounts annually. All shareholders receive a copy of these accounts.

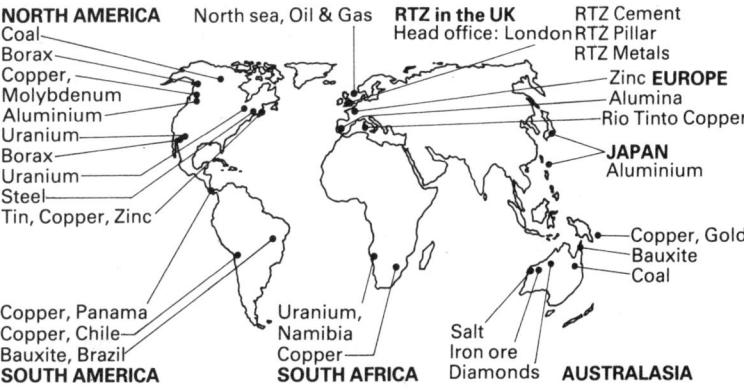

Major RTZ group operations. Very large public limited companies such as RTZ (Rio-Tinto-Zinc) often have operations in many different countries. Firms like these are called multi-nationals

A Public Limited Company enjoys **limited liability**. This means that shareholders are protected if the company fails to make a profit. They can only lose the money invested in the company, and cannot be held liable for the company's debts. People owed money by the firm, called **creditors**, can only claim on the assets (property and money owned by the firm). This reduces the shareholder's risk.

Since 1979, the government has encouraged more people to become shareholders as **nationalised industries** have been 'sold-off', and so become **privatised**.

Workshop   Workshop   Workshop

1 Explain what is meant by:
   (a) Assets
   (b) Shareholders
   (c) An entrepreneur
   (d) Creditors

2 How would you distinguish between the following:
   (a) A sole proprietor and a partnership
   (b) A private joint stock company and a public limited company?

3 The letters PLC appear after many firms' names. What do these stand for? Look through newspapers, packaging, on television and anywhere else that you are likely to see these initials and collect a list of the names of PLCs. What goods or services are they connected with?

4 Imagine that you want to set up your own business. What goods would you produce, or which services would you provide? What equipment would you need? How could you raise the money to start the business?

19

Size of firms

How firms grow

A successful profit-making firm may expand by putting some of its profits back into the company – by investing in up-to-date equipment or by building a larger factory, for example.

The firm could create extra shares for sale to investors, which would provide the company with extra money for growth. This is risky, however. Investors have to be confident of the firm's future success before they will part with their money.

A more convenient way for a company to expand is through a **merger**, that is, two firms coming together to form a single larger company (Cadbury-Schweppes, for example).

Alternatively, a firm may gain control of another firm by buying a sufficient number of shares to effect a **take-over**. The firm which has been taken over may be swallowed up by the larger company, or it may keep its identity. 1985 and 1986 saw a great deal of take-over activity – for example, Burton clothes retailers took over Debenhams, and Bell's Whisky distillers were taken over by Guinness.

The advantages of large firms

1. If one firm merges with another that sells the same kind of product, it will get a larger **market share**. This may lead to increased profits.

2. If a firm merges with another that sells a different product or a wider range of products, it may **diversify**, that is, produce a wider range of products. This is a help if one business activity goes into decline – for example, Ladbrokes, the bookmakers, also deal in package holidays.

3. A large firm is more likely to be able to buy raw materials more cheaply in bulk, to invest in research operations and to be able to transport finished products more efficiently. This results in **economies of scale**.

Burton expanded by taking over other firms involved in the retail trade, such as Debenhams

'Dear old Freddie – he's been merging Guinness and Distillers for years...'

Mergers between firms in the drinks industry have been a controversial feature of the 1980s

4 More efficient methods of production can be used: for example, mechanisation and automation may now be afforded to speed up production and cut manufacturing costs.

How do we measure a company's size?

- By counting the size of the work-force.
- By totalling the value of all the shares.
- By studying the amount of money it uses in a year (its **turnover**) and the profit it makes.

A government body, The Monopolies and Mergers Commission, commonly known as the Monopolies Commission, has powers to recommend that a merger should or should not be allowed to go ahead. The fear about mergers is that public choice may be limited and prices may rise. In such cases a merger may not be permitted because it would be 'against the public interest'.

Workshop   Workshop   Workshop

1 What does an economist mean by:
   (a) Merger
   (b) Take-over
   (c) Diversify
   (d) Market share?

2 Name three ways of estimating a firm's size.

3 Explain what the Monopolies and Mergers Commission does.

4 Read the passage 'BHS deal puts City in fever', adapted from a *Guardian* article, then answer the questions which follow.

BHS deal puts City in fever

Merger fever hit the City yesterday with news of two proposed multi-billion pound deals. British Home Stores and Habitat Mothercare announced an agreed £1.5 billion merger in the latest of a series of links which are changing the face of British retailing.

Imperial Group, the Players cigarettes, Courage beers and Golden Wonder crisps combine, and Britain's biggest biscuits firm, United Biscuits, added to the wave of takeover activity on the stock market by disclosing that they hoped to agree a £2.8 billion merger.

Imperial and United Biscuits would create a business with sales of more than £6 billion.

The BHS and Habitat Mothercare deal would create a group with yearly sales of £1 billion and 20,000 employees. It would link nearly 130 stores best known for lighting and clothing products with the Habitat Mothercare group which includes Richard Shops, Now and Heals.

(a) The 'City' refers mainly to the Stock Exchange where shares are bought and sold. Name the firms involved in the two mergers which put the City 'in fever'.

(b) What common activities are the two pairs of companies involved in?

(c) Which deal would create the most valuable company?

(d) What advantages and disadvantages may result for the companies' employees and for consumers from the British Home Stores and Habitat Mothercare deal?

Unit Eleven
The costs of production

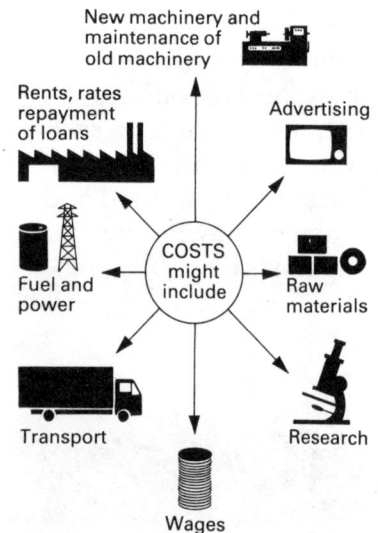

New machinery and maintenance of old machinery

Rents, rates repayment of loans

Advertising

COSTS might include

Fuel and power

Raw materials

Transport

Research

Wages

Entrepreneurs go into business to make a profit. This is called 'the profit motive'. But what is a profit?

REVENUE − COSTS = PROFIT

Simply, it is the difference between the money a firm makes from selling its goods or services, and the costs the company has had to pay out during production.

We can identify different types of **costs**.

FIXED COSTS have to be met whether or not the firm produces anything at all – for example, rents, **rates**, repayment of loans and the interest on borrowing.

VARIABLE COSTS alter according to the scale or level of production. These costs could include wages, raw materials and charges for fuel and power.

FIXED COSTS	+	VARIABLE COSTS	=	TOTAL COST
TOTAL COST	÷	NUMBER OF GOODS PRODUCED	=	AVERAGE COST OF EACH ARTICLE

After the firm has calculated the AVERAGE COST of producing each article they can then add on their profit before selling it. Firms try to keep their production costs down in order to maintain high levels of profits. When a finished product is sold, the money that the sale brings in is called **revenue**.

The firm receives the revenue and is able to pay for the various costs of production. If the costs have been underestimated or the finished article has sold for less

Transport is a major cost of production

than the expected price, then COSTS may exceed REVENUE. The result is a LOSS. If losses continue and the firm fails to make a profit, it may be forced into **liquidation** and so go out of business.

In order to reduce costs and increase profits, firms often try to achieve higher levels of **productivity**.

OUTPUT ÷ NUMBER OF WORKERS = PRODUCTIVITY

In the 1980s many British firms have reduced their number of workers in an attempt to cut costs and improve productivity. Increasing competition from abroad and shrinking world markets for British goods have forced firms to introduce more efficient methods of production, for example, robots and automated machinery. This has been one cause of the present high level of unemployment.

New technology has reduced the demand for workers in many industries

Workshop   Workshop   Workshop

1 What do you understand by:
   (a) Profit motive
   (b) Costs
   (c) Revenue
   (d) Productivity?

2 Explain why you think that profits are important to firms.

3 A market gardener grows tomatoes. His costs for a year are as follows:

Interest paid on bank loans taken out for:	£
transport	
irrigation system	
glasshouses	4 500
Compost	500
Fertiliser	150
Seed	100
Fuel for heating glasshouses	2 250
Wages	10 000

   (a) What are the market gardener's total costs?
   (b) Which of the costs are fixed, and which are variable?
   (c) If 17 000 kilos of tomatoes are produced in a year, how much would have to be charged for the market gardener just to cover his/her costs?
   (d) If there was a glut of tomatoes and the price fell to 50p per kilo, what would be the effect on the market gardener?
   (e) If there was a shortage, and the price rose to £2 per kilo, what would be the effect then?

23

Unit Twelve
How the government helps us

If you had been born a century ago, your chances of surviving through to adulthood would have been only fair.

Despite major advances in medical discoveries in the hundred years up to the late 1940s, the number of deaths from curable diseases was appalling, often because poor people could not afford to pay for the doctor's services, medicines or treatment in hospital.

The Labour government of 1945–51 believed that medical care should be free to everybody, rich and poor alike. So they created the National Health Service to provide this 'free' service, paid for through our taxes and National Insurance contributions.

Our taxes help to pay for this hospital – in return we get 'free' medical care

Maternity Benefit & Allowance	
Child Allowance (from 0 - School leaving age)	DEFENCE
Education, Libraries, Subsidised Theatres, arts, etc.	
Grants for students in higher education	ENVIRONMENTAL SERVICES – WATER, SEWAGE, PARKS
Y.T.S. Schemes	
Family Income Supplement, Free school meals, Supplementary Benefit (milk, vitamins)	LAW & ORDER + PROTECTIVE SERVICES
Unemployment Benefit 16 – 60 or 16 – 65, Sickness Benefit	ROADS + TRANSPORT
Invalidity Pension, Mobility Allowance, Attendance Allowance, Industrial Disablement Benefit	HEALTH (MEDICAL & DENTAL)
Pensions (men over 65 women over 60)	TRADE, INDUSTRY + EMPLOYMENT
Death Grant	

LIFELONG SUPPORT IN

'From the cradle to the grave'

At first prescriptions, dentures and spectacles were also free, but today charges are made for these unless you are a child, a pensioner or on a low income.

This is just one of many parts the government has played in taking care of the nation 'from the cradle to the grave', through the Welfare State.

The chart on the left shows just a few of the ways in which you can benefit from government help during your lifetime. Can you think of others?

The government also supports the nation in many other ways, for example through the Civil Service and by lending money to nationalised industries.

Help is not just confined to Britain. The government gives or lends money to poorer countries around the world.

Workshop　Workshop　Workshop

1　What do you understand by:
   (a) Pension
   (b) The Welfare State
   (c) Environmental services
   (d) National Health Service?

2　List the types of benefits to which people may be entitled during their lifetime.

3　Why do you think that the government is responsible for defence and law and order in modern times?

4　Study the diagram 'How the government will spend its money in 1986–7' then answer the questions which follow:

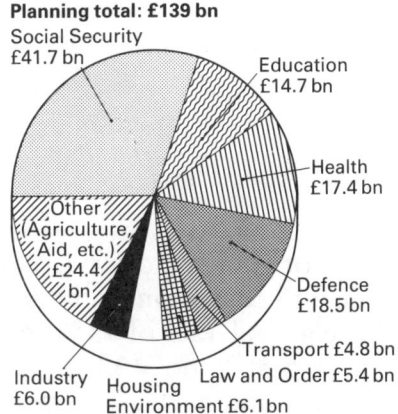

How the government will spend its money in 1986–7

   (a) What is Social Security?
   (b) What is the total amount that the government plans to spend?
   (c) Which is the largest individual amount?
   (d) What is this amount to be spent on?
   (e) How much is to be spent on education and what is its order of rank?
   (f) Approximately what proportion represents direct help to the people?

How your money helps the State

People often take the services and benefits provided by the State for granted and complain bitterly about the taxes they have to pay. If the government did not raise money by taxing our income and most of the goods we buy, then it would be unable to finance the many services which it makes available to all citizens.

Income tax

Income tax is charged on the money you earn. In Britain it is a progressive tax – in other words, the more you earn, the more you pay. But you do not pay tax on all your income. Everyone has a tax allowance, an amount of money they can earn which is not taxed.

Tax is calculated from income tax returns. A form is sent out by the Inland Revenue, the government department responsible for collecting income tax. From the information you supply, the Inland Revenue can calculate your allowance and the amount of tax to be paid on the remainder of your income. This remainder is known as *taxable income*.

Most employees have income tax deducted by their employer. This system is called PAYE (Pay As You Earn).

Value Added Tax

Value Added Tax or VAT is a tax that is added to the price of goods and services. It is collected at the point of sale and passed on to the Inland Revenue. Most goods have a VAT rate of 15%, but certain items are zero-rated, that is, no VAT is charged. These goods include food, children's clothes, books, newspapers, public transport, medicines supplied on prescriptions, and coal, gas and electricity.

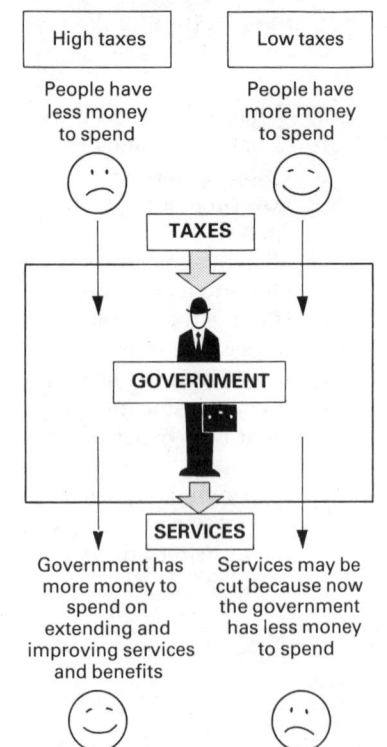

High taxes — People have less money to spend

Low taxes — People have more money to spend

TAXES

GOVERNMENT

SERVICES

Government has more money to spend on extending and improving services and benefits

Services may be cut because now the government has less money to spend

"I wouldn't mind so much if he had a TV licence!"

Workshop　　Workshop　　Workshop

1 Why does the government need taxes?

2 From the information in this Unit, suggest the taxes which might be paid by these people:
   (a) Sally Brown – bank clerk, car owner, smoker, takes a foreign holiday once a year.
   (b) Margaret Black – housewife, plays bingo, occasional drinker, owns a television.
   (c) James Green – farmer, drives a Land-Rover, shareholder in British Telecom, owns two gun dogs and shoots pheasants.

3 What are the possible advantages and disadvantages of increasing excise duties on alcohol and tobacco?

4 Why do think that VAT is not collected on food?

5 Read the passage 'Taxman "ignores" black economy', adapted from a *Guardian* article, then answer the following questions:
   (a) What does the term 'black economy' mean?
   (b) What is the difference between 'ghosts' and 'moonlighters'?
   (c) What has happened to firms that have been 'harassed and coerced' by the Inland Revenue?
   (d) Why do most firms agree to a settlement with the Inland Revenue?

Taxman 'ignores' black economy
By Andrew Rawnsley

BRITAIN is fast becoming a nation on the fiddle, riddled with moonlighters, double-jobbers and cowboy firms, according to the authors of a report published yesterday on the black economy.

Ghosts are people whose activities the tax authorities simply do not know about; moonlighters are those doing extra work, usually for cash in hand, on top of their normal jobs.

The National Federation of Self-Employed and Small Businesses says that while the Inland Revenue "harasses and coerces" small businessmen it is ignoring much more wide-spread abuses which are undermining the legitimate businesses of its members.

Some businesses, the federation suggests, are bankrupted as a result. Most agree to a settlement, not because it is a fair assessment of their profits, but to get the revenue off their backs.

Unit Fourteen
Inflation

How many times have you heard your parents or grandparents voicing similar complaints?

'When I was young you could buy a tub of ice-cream for a penny ....' 'It used to cost 17p to catch the bus into town, it's 55p now!'

These price rises are caused by **inflation**. Inflation is a general rise in prices – when the majority of prices go up. If prices rise then our money will not go as far and we will need more money to buy the things we usually buy. So inflation reduces the value of our money.

Sometimes, even during periods of inflation, the price of certain goods can stay the same or even fall. Can you think of any examples of this happening?

Changes in prices are sometimes referred to as changes in the cost of living. The government measures these changes in the **Retail Price Index**. Each month the government conducts a survey of the prices of the same goods and services used by a typical family. By adding together all the price rises over a twelve-month period, the government can calculate the percentage change over the year.

Rises in the price of oil can have a major effect on inflation

Why do prices rise?

There are many different reasons for inflation, some of which are very complex. If it was simple to cure inflation, then it might not be such a major problem for governments all over the world.

Some of the major causes of inflation are:

1 Increased costs of fuels and raw materials – Britain needs to import large quantities of these from other countries. If the price of these raw materials increases, then British firms will have to pass their increased costs on to the consumer in the form of higher prices.
2 Workers may demand higher wages in order to maintain their living standards. These increases will again have to be passed on to the consumer.
3 As we saw in Unit Six, where demand is greater than supply, prices rise. For example, in South-East England where there is a shortage of building land and large numbers of people wish to buy houses, house prices are higher than in other parts of the country.
4 When governments spend more than they receive in tax revenue, they have to borrow to make up the difference. High levels of borrowing can cause inflation.

Workshop　Workshop　Workshop

1 If the annual rate of inflation was ten per cent, how much would the following items cost in a year's time:
   (a) A take-away meal presently costing £3
   (b) A portable television costing £180
   (c) A new car which is now sold for £6 500?

2 Find out through newspapers or news broadcasts, the present rate of inflation. Is the rate going up, down or remaining stable?

3 Study the graphs. Note that they show percentage changes from year to year. Use the information shown to say whether the following statements are TRUE or FALSE.

Average earnings represent total income, including overtime payments

(a) Over the period 1981–85, changes in average earnings have been greater than those of retail prices.
(b) People in work are now better off.
(c) At the end of 1981 earnings rose more slowly than retail prices.
(d) People were better off because of this.

Unit Fifteen
The Budget and economic growth

The member of the government responsible for economic policy is the Chancellor of the Exchequer. In March each year he presents his Budget. This is a statement made to the House of Commons, in which the Chancellor outlines:

1 How the economy has progressed during the past twelve months.
2 The main changes proposed in government spending.
3 How he or she plans to raise money, through changes in taxes and government borrowing.

Budget Day is therefore very important both to economists and to ordinary citizens. It tells us how much tax we will have to pay and how much benefit we are entitled to.

The government, through its economic policies, tries to bring about improvements in people's standards of living. This can only happen if the country produces more goods and services, leading to higher incomes for workers, higher profits for firms and extra tax revenue for the government. This is known as economic growth.

How economic growth is achieved

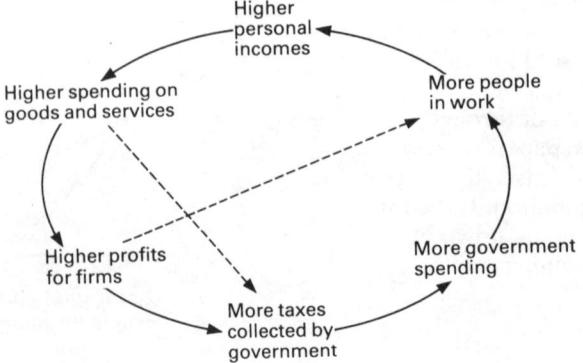

Economic growth has led us to expect better housing, hospitals, roads, shopping centres and schools. People can now treat as necessities goods which were once regarded as luxuries. As a result, living standards have risen dramatically. Whether working or unemployed, most people expect to live comfortably and own a wide range of consumer goods, which include a car, colour television, washing machine and similar 'luxuries'.

Economic growth has enabled people to buy many more luxury goods for their homes, thereby raising living standards

What are the costs of growth?

Although we need economic growth to provide jobs and to maintain living standards, some people argue that growth uses up scarce materials — we are consuming natural resources such as oil and gas which cannot be replaced. Some natural resources — for example, fishing and forestry — may be over-exploited. Pollution of the environment can be caused by factories, power stations and vehicle exhaust fumes. Critics of economic growth hold that such 'costs of growth' will lead to disaster in the long run, affecting the lives of generations to come.

Workshop   Workshop   Workshop

1 Who is the present Chancellor of the Exchequer, and where is his official London residence?

2 Why is the Budget important to the ordinary citizen?

3 Why is economic growth regarded as essential by most economists?

4 Compare the photographs of living rooms in the 1950s and 1980s and list the differences between them. Explain why living standards have changed in the last thirty years.

5 Discuss with your teacher some of the 'costs of growth' which can be seen in the world today. What are the causes of these problems? Is economic growth worth the risks that we take?

Unit Sixteen
Local government spending

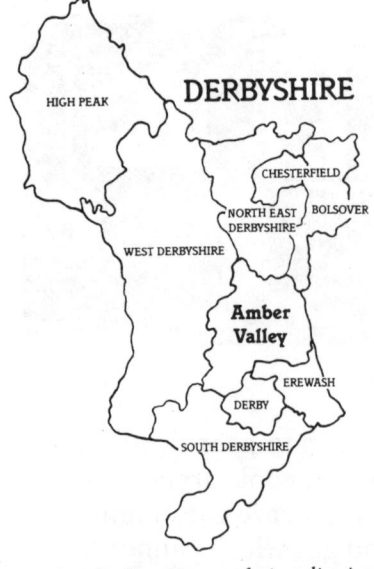

Amber Valley is one of nine district councils in the county of Derbyshire

What do the local councils provide for you?

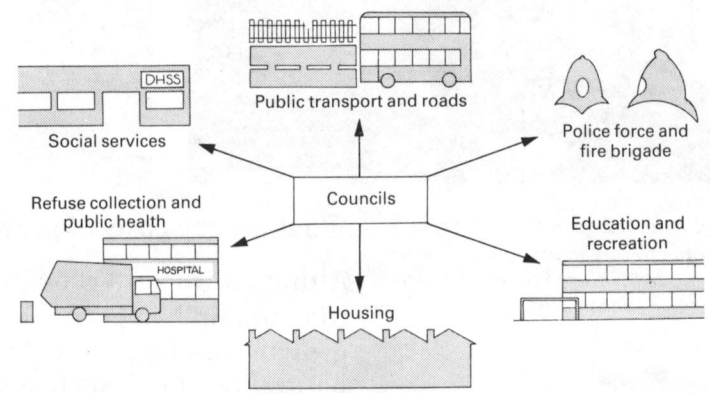

Social services

Public transport and roads

Police force and fire brigade

Refuse collection and public health

Councils

Education and recreation

Housing

The system of local government in Britain depends upon where you live. Large city areas such as London, Birmingham, Liverpool, Manchester, Sheffield, Leeds and Newcastle are run by city councils, while the surrounding areas are run by district councils (borough councils around the City of London). Away from these areas in the 'shire' counties, local government is run on two levels, by county councils and district councils.

Case Study 1: Derbyshire County Council

Derbyshire County Council provides services for almost 900 000 people. Its two main sources of income are taxpayers and ratepayers. Central government gives a grant, raised through income tax, to DCC to pay for almost half its spending. A similar amount of money is collected from the owners of houses and business premises in the form of rates. Rates are a local property tax. The bigger and better the property, the more you pay in rates. They are administered and collected by the district councils. A large proportion of the rates are then passed on to the county council and spent in the ways shown on Chart A.

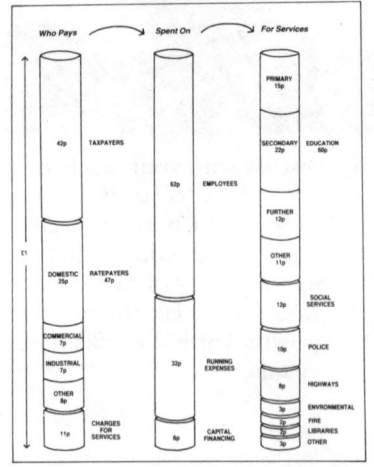

Chart A

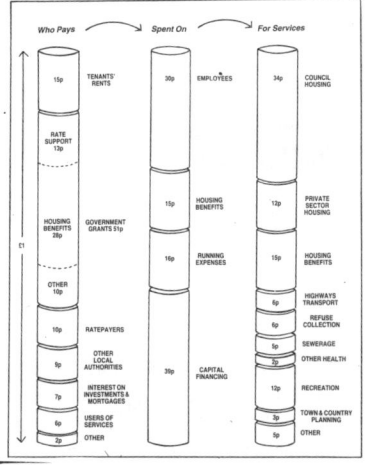

AMBER VALLEY DISTRICT COUNCIL
Where each pound comes from and how it is spent

Chart B

Case Study 2: Amber Valley District Council

Amber Valley is one of nine district councils in Derbyshire, serving a smaller area than the county council and providing for local needs (see Chart B).

By looking at Charts A and B, compare the different services provided by Derbyshire County Council and Amber Valley District Council.

Local councils may also borrow

Some local authorities pay for new buildings by borrowing. They sell bonds to individual citizens and to financial institutions such as banks. You have to leave your money with them for a specific length of time, during which it earns interest. At the end of this period, the bond is cashed in.

Workshop   Workshop   Workshop

1 Is the area you live in run by a district council, a county council and a district council, a city council or a London borough council? Name your local authority (or authorities).

2 Study Chart A and Chart B.
   A *(i)* What proportion of Derbyshire County Council's spending is on wages?
      (ii) What percentage of county council spending is on education?
      (iii) What are 'domestic ratepayers'?

   B *(i)* What is the most expensive service provided by the District Council?
      (ii) What sorts of services would be provided under recreation?

WEST YORKSHIRE Metropolitan County Council
Bonds **11%** 4–8 YEARS
Minimum £500. Interest (subject to tax changes 6th April 1986) payable half yearly. Explanatory leaflets and application form from: Director of Finance, County Hall, Wakefield, West Yorksire WF1 2QN. Telephone: Wakefield 367111, extn 2685.

Local authorities often advertise their new issues of bonds in the national newspapers. Note: Under local government reorganisation, West Yorkshire, like the other five metropolitan county councils and the Greater London Council, was abolished from the end of March 1986. However, even after their abolition, these councils will continue to pay interest to those people who have lent them money.

3 *(a)* Look at the advertisement for bonds in West Yorkshire Metropolitan County Council. Explain what is meant by 'Bonds 11% 4–8 years'.
   (b) What is the minimum amount of money that you could lend to West Yorkshire Metropolitan County Council?
   (c) How often is interest paid on your loan?

4 In future, rates will be replaced by a 'community charge'. All people over 18 will pay, not just home owners. What are the advantages and disadvantages of this reform?

33

Britain's imports and exports

One measure of Britain's economic health is its ability to 'pay its way in the world'. This involves the study of:

IMPORTS – goods and services produced elsewhere and bought in this country.
EXPORTS – goods and services produced in this country and sold in other countries.

Why do we trade?

Trade takes place for a number of reasons:
1   Basic raw materials which are not found in this country have to be imported.
2   We cannot grow all the food we need, due to the British climate and land shortage.
3   We may not be able to produce enough of a manufactured good to satisfy demand.
4   Countries specialise in producing those goods which they can make most cheaply and efficiently. If we are able to import goods more cheaply than we can produce them, then we will do so. In return, we will export those goods in which we have the advantage.
5   Trading gives a wider variety of choice to consumers.

Most bulky imports and exports travel by sea

TABLE 1   Britain's trading partners, 1983 (percentages)

	EXPORTS	IMPORTS
EEC	44	46
Rest of Western Europe	12.5	16
North America	15.5	14
Other developed countries	5	8
Oil-exporting countries	10	4
Other developing countries	11	10
Centrally planned economies (communist countries)	2	2
Total	100	100

We have a greater amount of choice because of trade

What do we import and export?

Until the 1970s, Britain imported mainly food and raw materials. It exported manufactured goods to pay for its imports. Its ability as a manufacturing nation led to the country being called 'the workshop of the world'. However, Britain's manufacturing industry has declined rapidly in recent years. Now, more manufactured goods are imported than exported. On the other hand, Britain now produces more of its own food, and is self-sufficient in oil since the North Sea oilfields began production in the late 1970s.

TABLE 2   Britain's trade, 1983 (to nearest whole percentage point)

	EXPORTS	IMPORTS
Food, beverages and tobacco	7	12
Raw materials	3	7
Fuels	22	11
Manufactured goods	66	68
Others	2	2
Total	100	100

Workshop   Workshop   Workshop

1   What are:
   (a) Exports
   (b) Imports?

2   Explain why Britain needs to trade with other countries.

3   From the figures given in Table 1:
   (a) What percentages of Britain's exports and imports are traded with European countries?
   (b) Why do you think that trade with Europe has increased rapidly in the last twenty years?
   (c) Draw a bar graph to show the information in Table 1. Draw separate bars for imports and exports for each country.

4   From the information in Table, 2, draw pie charts to show the main commodities Britain exports and imports. Draw separate charts for exports and imports.

Unit Eighteen
The importance of international trade

Examples of Britain's visible trade

The import and export of goods between countries is known as **visible trade**, because the goods can be seen to be moving.

In 1983, the value of Britain's visible trade in exports was £60 534 millions. The total value of imports came to £65 993 million. The difference between the totals of imported and exported goods is called the **balance of trade**. Therefore Britain had a trade **deficit**, or loss, of £5 459 million. If we had exported more than we imported, we would have had a surplus, or profit, on the balance of trade.

Trade is not just concerned with the movement of goods around the world. Countries also trade in services and money. Britain has come to depend more and more on the revenue received for services provided (for example, in tourism, banking, insurance and international transportation). British firms also invest overseas, which is repaid with interest. This form of trading is known as **invisible trade** – no actual goods are exchanged.

To get a complete record of Britain's trading we therefore have to compare the total values of both visible and invisible imports and exports. These figures are known as the **balance of payments**.

Balance of payments figures are published monthly in Britain, giving economists and the government an accurate idea of how the country is performing, compared with its trading partners.

Some countries are able to produce certain goods more cheaply than their competitors due to lower production costs or higher levels of technology and skills. Japan is a modern example of such a nation.

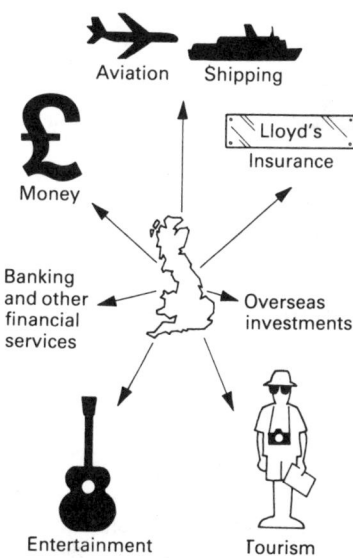

Examples of Britain's invisible export trade

- Aviation
- Shipping
- Money
- Lloyd's Insurance
- Banking and other financial services
- Overseas investments
- Entertainment
- Tourism

Free trade or protection?

When a country finds that it is continually importing more than it is exporting and showing an unhealthy balance of payments, calls may be made for the protection of home industries. There are two main ways to protect trade:

TARIFFS – taxes put on imports to increase their price artificially

QUOTAS – limits placed on the quantities of goods that may be imported

Free trade, it is argued, would mean the closure of firms and large-scale loss of jobs. But there are strong arguments in its favour:

- Greater choice for consumers.
- Cheaper goods are available in the shops, leading to higher standards of living.
- Good trading relationships with other countries – protection could lead to retaliation by other nations; they could refuse to import the protected nation's goods.

Workshop   Workshop   Workshop

1 Explain the difference between:
   (a) visible and invisible trade
   (b) 'balance of trade' and 'balance of payments'.

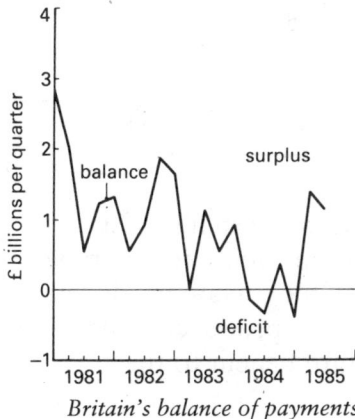

Britain's balance of payments

2 Look at the graph 'Britain's balance of payments', then answer the following questions.

   (a) Is Britain's balance of payments stable or does it fluctuate (move up and down)?
   (b) When did the value of exports equal the value of imports?
   (c) Which was the worst year for Britain's balance of payments?
   (d) Would you say Britain's balance of payments was healthy during the 1981–85 period? Give a reason for your answer.

   (e) You will remember that Britain had a balance of trade deficit in 1983. Compare the balance of payments graph for the same period and comment on your findings.

3 In your kitchen at home make a list of as many foreign goods as you can find and a list of British goods. Compare and discuss your lists in class.

4 Should we limit imports coming into this country? Give reasons for your answer.

Unit Nineteen
Economic systems

In the world today economic systems are based on two broad types:

TYPES	PLANNED ECONOMY	MARKET ECONOMY
MAIN FEATURES	The State decides: • What and how much is to be produced. • Wage rates for workers. • Prices in the shops.	• Consumers decide, by their spending habits, what private businesses produce. • Prices and wages are determined by supply and demand.
ADVANTAGES	1 Everyone has a right to work. 2 Government ensures that everyone has a fair share of the national wealth.	1 Less administration needed at government level. 2 Firms produce goods which people want. 3 Consumers have a greater freedom of choice.
DISADVANTAGES	1 Limited freedom of choice for consumers. 2 Mistakes or poor organisation by planners may lead to waste.	1 Great divisions develop between the rich and poor. 2 Markets are affected by 'booms' and 'slumps' leading to unemployment.
BEST EXAMPLES	USSR	USA

No pure examples of these economic systems exist. Countries find it impossible to keep totally to one type of system. For example, in the USSR private producers exist to meet local demand for farm produce, while in the USA the State provides welfare benefit to the unemployed.

PUBLIC SECTOR
Controlled by: government, nationalised industries, local authorities

25%

75%

PRIVATE SECTOR
Firms and businesses controlled by companies or individuals

The British economy

The sale of shares in British Telecom has been one of the biggest privatisation schemes in the 1980s

Many countries have a *mixed economy* by taking parts of each of the two major economic systems.

The British economy is based mainly on the market system. However, as you will have seen in earlier units, the government has a major role to play in the provision of some goods and services.

Public or private companies?

After the Second World War, many important industries were nationalised. That is they were taken over and run by the State. Such a policy is favoured by the Labour party.

During the 1980s, Conservative party policy has been to sell publicly owned firms back to the private sector. This is known as **privatisation**. The money raised has helped to pay for government spending instead of having to increase levels of taxes or government borrowing.

Privatisation has been criticised for several reasons:

1   The benefits of selling a profitable industry are only short-term; future profits are lost to the government.
2   If newly privatised firms are run solely for profit, services to the public may be cut.
3   Critics have accused the government of selling the industries for too little.

As a result of privatisation, the public sector is gradually getting smaller. However, it will not disappear altogether because the private sector will not want to take over non-profit-making industries and services.

The privatisation of public transport is designed to create more competition between firms. It is claimed that this will bring about a cheaper and more efficient system.

Workshop   Workshop   Workshop

1   What kind of economy does Britain have?

2   Which of the two major economic systems would you prefer to live in? Give your reasons.

3   What is privatisation?

4   Which of the following services would governments be unlikely to transfer to the private sector? Give a reason for each choice.

(a)   Bus services
(b)   Defence
(c)   Health services
(d)   Police
(e)   State television service
(f)   Coal-mining industry

Unit Twenty
Economic development

This book has concentrated on Britain, an economically developed nation and part of the rich 'North'. The majority of people in the world today live in the developing and underdeveloped countries of the poor 'South'. The table shows the main features of these countries.

UNDER-DEVELOPED (Third World)	DEVELOPING (Second World)	DEVELOPED (First World)
• Low incomes • Little paid employment • Low level of technical knowledge and skills • Few roads and railways • Poor diet • Poor-quality housing • Few medical services • Low life expectancy • Few city dwellers	As countries develop they become richer. Their workers learn new skills, more goods are produced and they receive higher wages. Therefore their standards of living improve. People start to move from the country to the towns and cities.	• High incomes • Large numbers of wage-earners • High level of technical knowledge and skills • Good transport and communications systems • High standard of living, diet, housing and health care, leading to longer life expectancy • Large numbers live in towns and cities

What problems do developing and underdeveloped nations face?

A characteristic feature of these nations is a 'vicious circle of poverty'. Breaking out of such a circle is a real problem. The gap between the developed nations and

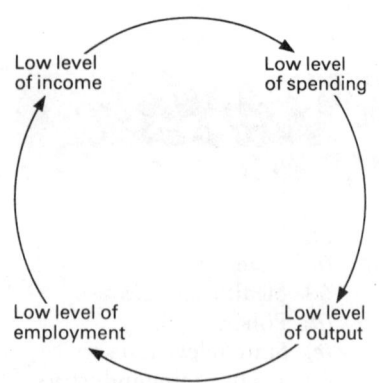

A vicious circle of poverty

Low level of income → Low level of spending → Low level of output → Low level of employment →

In 1985–86, millions of £s were raised in Britain through Live Aid, Band Aid and Sport Aid

Foreign aid can help speed up development projects

the rest of the world is widening all the time. Generally, the problems for poor countries are:

- scarce resources
- a rapidly rising population
- barriers which slow down development – for example, religious beliefs or extreme political viewpoints
- large gaps between rich and poor people
- lack of money for new investment
- lack of jobs

Help from outside

In some cases outside help may be available. Countries which had large empires, such as Britain and France, maintain close links with their former colonies. Foreign aid in the form of grants (gifts of money or goods) and loans (usually at low rates of interest) is often given. These can be used to improve agriculture and to provide jobs through building new factories.

It may seem that the poor countries of the South depend totally on those of the rich North. This is not so. While developed countries export manufactured goods, they also need many raw materials and foodstuffs produced in the underdeveloped and developing nations. Therefore both rich and poor nations depend on each other.

Workshop   Workshop   Workshop

1   Explain the term 'a Third World country'.

2   In your own words, explain how underdeveloped countries differ from developed countries.

3   Aid is also given to Third World countries by voluntary organisations. Find out the names of as many of these as you can. Send off for further information about their activities. Your teacher should be able to provide you with some addresses to write to.

4   In these days of high unemployment, some people argue that we should help ourselves rather than give millions of pounds in overseas aid to the poorer nations of the world. Do you agree or disagree with this? Discuss your point of view with the rest of the class.

Unit Twenty One
Writing an economics project

Choice of subject
Your first job is to decide on a topic. You must remember that your project has to be connected with the world of economics. The topic 'What it is like to be unemployed' would be no use, but a survey of unemployment in your area would be.

Make sure you choose a topic where finding information is not too difficult.

The title needs to be clearly expressed and should explain the objective of the project: for example 'A survey of unemployment in my neighbourhood'.

Structure of the project
Structure is *very* important. A project should not be written in a haphazard manner. It will require thought, discussion and planning. If possible, it should be organised to fit a particular pattern.

The following can be used as a useful guideline:

1 Question/Statement: e.g. Unemployment in my neighbourhood
2 Observe and collect information (or data)
3 Present the data
4 Interpret the data
5 Come to a conclusion

Collecting information
Collect and record your data carefully and accurately. You may be given some basic information by your teacher. Where can you find the extra information which will make your project stand out from the rest?

(i) Look in your school/college library under the appropriate section.
(ii) Go to your local library – tell the librarian the subject you're studying and you'll be shown the section containing useful information. Take brief notes; some books are marked 'reference' and cannot be removed from the library.
(iii) Up-to-date information may also be found in newspapers and magazines. Cut out articles and pictures and file them away for later use.
(iv) Depending upon the subject matter of your topic, it might be helpful to collect leaflets and information from banks, building societies or firms. You will find the addresses in *Yellow Pages*.

Writing the project
Having collected your data, it must then be presented. There are various ways of doing this such as a line graph, chart, pie graph.

Check that:
1 Your facts are correct – keep checking with original sources.
2 You have explained the subject matter so that it can be clearly understood.
3 You have related your writing to some economic ideas or theory.

Go for originality, use your own words, avoid copying directly from books. If you do use someone else's words, say whose they are and where you took the information from.

By the time you finish you should have a greater understanding of the issue you have chosen, and of how much economics influences our everyday lives.

Word Check

balance of payments: the difference in the values of a country's imports and exports, both visible and invisible.

balance of trade: the difference between the values of all the goods imported and exported by a country.

consumer: anyone who buys and uses goods and/ or services.

costs: all the items paid for by a firm when it produces goods or services.

credit: buying goods or services now, while paying for them some time in the future.

creditors: individuals or companies who are owed money.

deficit: a shortage of money caused by spending that is higher than income.

diversify: to produce a wider range or variety of goods and services.

earnings: the total amount earned by a worker, that is the basic wage plus any additional payments such as overtime and bonuses.

economies of scale: savings achieved through a firm producing at a high level of output.

entrepreneur: anyone who runs a business; the two main features are taking risks and coping with uncertainty.

inflation: a rise in the general level of prices, accompanied by a fall in the general value of money.

interest: the cost of borrowing, and a reward for those who lend money.

invisible trade: trade mainly in services (rather than goods) including tourism.

limited liability: a reduction of the risks taken by shareholders. If the firm in which they invest their money goes into liquidation, they stand to lose only the money that they have actually invested.

liquidation: when a firm is unable to pay its way and is forced to sell off its assets (buildings, machinery, lorries etc.) to pay its creditors; that is, it is forced to go out of business.

loss: a firm makes a loss when costs are greater than revenue.

market forces: demand and supply determining prices.

market share: the proportion of the market which one individual firm supplies.

merger: where two firms join together to form one large company.

nationalised industries: major industries owned by the State and managed by a board appointed by the government.

opportunity cost: the alternatives you have to do without when you decide how to spend your money.

piece-rate: payment for a worker based on the output produced by that worker.

privatisation: the sale of shares in nationalised industries to individuals and institutions.

productivity: a means of measuring the efficiency of a firm or industry – mainly calculated by dividing output by the number of workers employed.

profit: the result when a firm's revenue exceeds its costs.

rates: a local property tax to pay for the services provided by local councils.

retail price index: a measure of the rate at which the prices of goods and services change, from which the rate of inflation is calculated.

revenue: the income achieved by firms from the sales of their products.

salary: an amount earned by a worker per year – usually divided by twelve and received in equal monthly payments.

scale of preference: the order of importance in which consumers spend their money on goods and services.

shareholders: the owners of private and public limited companies.

take-over: the gaining of control by one firm over another.

time-rate: payment for a worker based on a unit of time; that is, an amount per hour, day or week.

trade unions: an organisation of workers set up to look after the interests (usually pay and working conditions) of their members.

turnover: the total amount of money a firm handles, usually in a year.

visible trade: imports and exports of goods (excluding all services).

wage/wage rate: the basic rate of pay without including overtime or any extra payments such as bonuses.

working population: the number of people aged between sixteen and sixty years (in the case of women) or sixty-five years (for men) who are able and available for work.